T5-BBQ-003

7
THINGS EVERY MOTHER SHOULD TEACH HER SON

For Every Woman Trying Hard to Be Mom & Dad

Author: **Darrell W. King**

Editor: **Quintrelle Griggs**

Publisher: **Get Knowledge Books**

PRINT ISBN   *(978-0-9974432-0-2) – Get Knowledge Books*
E-BOOK ISBN   *(978-0-9974432-1-9) – Get Knowledge Books*

About The Author

Darrell King is a minister, author, executive producer, mentor and former youth pastor with a deep passion for working with young people. As an executive producer, he has worked in the mainstream Christian music industry for over 20 years. He is also the author of the new book, *This Business of Christian Music*. As a mentor and youth pastor, King has been blessed to teach, motivate and minister to hundreds of young people. King is the founder and CEO of *(TMM) The Missing Man, Incorporated*, a 501c3 nonprofit established to encourage and support single mothers by helping to motivate and mentor their sons. He is married and currently lives in the Dallas, Texas area. To keep up with and learn more about Minister Darrell King, log onto *Facebook/darrell.king2*

THE FOREWORD

I've had the privilege of knowing Darrell King for almost four years now. We initially met when he agreed to help my sister with a project that God gave her to help raise money to offset the cost of mission expenses for church members who wanted to go on foreign mission trips. Since that time, he has become a member of my family. He's my BIL (brother-in-law).

One of the things that I admire about Darrell is that he is so knowledgeable about many different things. If you read the *About The Author* section, then you have somewhat of an idea of what I'm talking about. He is such a well-rounded individual. To me, Darrell is one of the best that God created. He's just a gem, precious and rare! He's a blessing to all that come in contact with him. You can't be around Darrell and value not be added to your life.

He is one of the kindest and most considerate men that I know. Not only does he think about other people, but he puts them before himself. If he can help you in any way, he will. In my opinion, he has the heart of God.

If you think **CHIVALRY** is dead, then you've never met Darrell King. He is the epitome of a Perfect Gentleman. On several occasions, I've witnessed him open doors for ladies as opposed to them having to open the doors for themselves. As you read Thing 1, "The Definition of a Woman," you will learn other gentlemanly qualities that Darrell exhibits.

As a youth pastor and teen mentor, Darrell learned that many single mothers desperately wanted to know what to do in order to raise a son that would be a decent, productive and law abiding citizen. As a mother, whether single or married, every topic discussed in *7 Things Every Mother Should Teach Her Son* addresses the vital role that you play in shaping your son into a well accomplished man. With God's help and applying what you read in this book, you can change the attitudes of the next generation of men. If you change the generation, then you can change the family unit.

Quintrelle Griggs

Acknowledgements

This book is dedicated to my mother, **Mrs. Debra Wilson**. I thank God for her having the courage and dedication to parent by her instincts. For every person who has commented on how good a man I am, the credit goes to God and my mother. This book is also dedicated to every mother, grandmother, aunt, sister, godmother, and all other females who have a responsibility to help raise a boy into a man

Table of Contents

~ *Bibliography* ~
(83)

Chapter One

MY INTRODUCTION

What can I do to help shape and mold my son into a decent man? As a youth pastor and teen mentor, I have been approached by many mothers asking me that question over the years. Some asked because they were not sure if their sons' current attitudes of disrespect and unruliness were temporary or signs of serious troubles to come. Others asked because they were worried that the absence of a supportive father figure in their sons' lives destined them to failure.

I do understand why so many mothers would ask that question. Observing the current state of pre-teen and teenage American boys today can be somewhat depressing.

Today's young men equate manhood to alcohol drinking, weed smoking, tattoos and body piercings. They embrace a disrespectful, unsympathetic and hard-core persona. They see nothing wrong with having children out of wedlock. They accept the idea of serving prison time and welcome run-ins with the police as badges of honor.

Many of them have a hustle mentality. Not to be confused with honest, hard work, their hustles are illegal. They oppose discipline. They lack self control and strive to achieve G or "gangster" status while opposing the ways of a civilized gentleman.

Our society of young males has no respect for the females they describe as "garden tools" and "female dogs." They are not inclined to open the door for a female or pull out her chair when dining at a restaurant. To them, women are nothing more than accessories put on earth to fulfill their sexual needs.

You would think this type of behavior should raise red flags. However, it does not.

A great percentage of our American society accepts this as normal male behavior. But what has become normal and acceptable behavior fuels the continuous degradation of our young American men.

A recent study by the United States Department of Justice concluded that men today are now over eight times more likely to be incarcerated than women. According to **Newser.com**, multi-ethnic male gang activity has increased in the last ten years. The Federal Bureau of Investigation's (FBI) recent yearly national gang crime reports are also citing an increase in gang activity by elementary school aged boys.

If this information is not disturbing enough, it seems the future of education for young men is equally bleak. National reports on the average American high school dropout rate show an 8 to thirteen percent increase in the number of male dropouts since the mid 1990s coast to coast.

EducationPortal.com recently shared a story based on several credible sources which detailed the occurrence of a declining number of American men to women attending and graduating from college.

The facts are clear. The commendable state of men is seemingly decreasing with every new generation. And I am sure every good mother with a son wonders how she can keep her son from being a bad statistic.

It is often said that it takes a man to raise a man, but I believe it takes a woman to raise a complete man. When it comes to the issue of raising a boy, I think men only have two distinct advantages over women. The first advantage is strength. Men are generally stronger than women physically. This often allows them to reinforce their fatherhood without fear of retaliation.

The second advantage is the fact that all men were once boys, therefore they know how boys think. But what men often struggle with is how to interpret what women are thinking about men.

And the fact that men normally don't think like a woman actually gives women an advantage when it comes to raising boys.

I preached a Mother's Day sermon one Sunday entitled "You Get It From Your Momma." My scriptural text came from First Kings 3. In the sermon I mentioned the fact that mothers are not perfect. They may not have the ability to teach their sons how to change tires, fix leaking pipes or hit baseballs, but they can teach them some very important lessons. These lessons can help their sons live in positive progression and put a dent into the current downward spiral of manhood in our society.

I have much respect for women who have to **woMAN up** and raise their children without the children's fathers. I'm certain this is not the plan of most mothers, but it is a reality for many of them today. As a mother with a son to raise, you have a choice.

You can hide behind the understandable excuse that you did not conceive your son alone and should not have to raise him alone, or you can roll up your sleeves, kick the excuses out the window and begin the task of teaching and training your son to be a contributing, civilly respectable man in our society.

This book is written to all women with sons but places an emphasis on those women who are trying to be mom and dad. While you can somewhat fill in for your son's dad at times, **you can never really be his dad**. Don't allow this fact to be a setback in your mission. I have witnessed many of the challenges that single mothers face when raising a boy alone. I know these challenges can be overcome. You have a tough job ahead but be encouraged. With the **7 Things** in this book and much prayer, **you can do it!**

FYI – You will find a section for notes after each (Thing) chapter. Use this section to write your thoughts and/or questions about what you have read.

Chapter Two
Thing 1

The Definition of a Woman

I will never forget the day my mom walked into my room without knocking and caught me gawking at the pictures of naked women. I was 10 years old and found some discarded *Playboy* magazines while outside playing. Feeling as though I had found a million dollars, I managed to stash the magazines under my shirt and sneak them into my room. Immediately I went from begging my mother to go outside to quietly staying in my room with the door closed every day. Although my mother was a single parent with an evening job and spent her days trying to catch up on her sleep, it did not take her long to realize that something was taking place in my room.

Caught red-handed, I was sure I was about to get the beating of a lifetime. My mother walked over to the bunk bed where I was sitting on the bottom bunk. She grabbed the magazine out of my hand and said, "I knew something was going on in here! So this is what has been keeping you in your room the last few days." As I braced myself for the beating that I knew was about to come, my mother surprised me by sitting down on the bed beside me. She opened one of the magazines, pointed at the vagina of one of the models and said, "This is a vagina." She continued by pointing at the model's breasts and said, "These are breasts. They are fun to look at, huh?" By this time I was very unsettled. "You want to see mine?" she asked.

After being asked that question, I experienced a mixture of emotions that I will never be able to explain. I did not know whether to scream or cry. "No!" I shouted. "Then why are you looking at theirs? Your sisters and I have breasts and vaginas." "This model," she pointed, "is someone's mother, sister or daughter."

"One day when you're an adult," she said, "you will find a special lady." "You and she will love one another. That's the ONLY woman you should feel comfortable looking at naked. Until you meet that woman, Darrell Wayne King, learn to respect the secrecies of the female anatomy."

After that, she dropped the magazine on the floor and left my room. I picked the magazine up but could not see the model in the same way. All I could think about was the model being someone's mother, sister or daughter! And I could not imagine a guy looking at my mother or sisters like that.

As an adult, that lesson has stayed with me. Through the years classmates, acquaintances and coworkers have sought my camaraderie through strip club invites or nude model texts or emails. I sternly and quickly informed them that I have no interest in such things.

This one simple lesson, taught to me in a unique way by my mother, shaped the way I view women today.

And with so many men adversely affected by porn addictions, I'm glad she did what she did. I see and respect women for more than what is underneath their clothes. I am not the guy that appreciates women who are exhibitionists. This is a lesson that only my mother could have taught me.

More young men are growing up with the wrong definition of what a woman is. They are comfortable at an early age identifying women as "Bitches" and "Hoes." They hear singers and rappers declare this in today's popular music. They even hear their female classmates and peers salute each other in this manner. I witnessed a 14 year old boy tell his 16 year old sister to "shut up bitch" during a playful moment in a church parking lot. She laughed and replied, "I am a bitch, and you better leave me alone before I show you."

Many people believe it is a man's job to teach a boy how to define the value of a woman. However, I believe a woman can do this better than a man. It's simple.

A mature woman knows how she wants a man to treat her. This gives a mother an advantage when it comes to teaching her son how to treat a woman.

So, how can you teach your son how to value and respect women? First, you should understand that your son is smarter and more alert than you may think. I have had numerous conversations with young boys, ages three to nine, who freely share with me the things that occurred in their homes.

Many of them would tell me about their mothers fighting with men or changing boyfriends often. One six year old woke up in his mom's bed only to witness his mom having sex with a man she just met that day. A four year old told me that a man, which he called by name, was constantly calling his mom's phone and scaring her. These were unsolicited conversations. I never asked the boys for this information.

A psychologist diagnosed one boy with a condition that causes aggressive behavior.

This stemmed from him feeling powerless to help his mother while observing her many fights with her boyfriend.

I knew most of the mothers of these boys well, and they trusted me as a youth mentor and pastor to be a positive role model for their sons. However, there was no way I could spend one or two days a month with these boys and compete with what they were witnessing in their homes on a daily basis.

This is the reason why mothers must be the main role models for their sons. If a boy repeatedly hears a man call his mother derogatory names without consequence or rebuttal, he will begin to accept that as being a normal way to address a woman. If a boy witnesses his mother casually sleeping with different men on a regular basis, that too will become acceptable behavior to him. If a boy knows his mother is living with a man out of wedlock, then his mother will be teaching him that marriage is not important.

More importantly, it is a proven fact according to **SafeHorizon.org** and **ClarkProsecutor.org** that if a boy witnesses constant acts of domestic violence against his mother, he is twice as likely to abuse women than boys who do not witness such acts.

Secondly, as a mother you must be careful of the people you trust around your son. Many women who are raising their sons alone feel that it is important to have male mentors around their sons as much as possible. I agree. However, you must keep in mind that every man will not qualify to be a mentor because every man does not respect women. This includes friends and family members. Just because your father, brother, uncle or neighbor is a man does not mean he is the best male to mentor your son.

Boys are very impressionable. Therefore, allowing them to spend even a little time with men who are players or womanizers will defeat your purpose to teach your son respect for women. It is important that you know as much about the character and mindset of any mentor you trust to spend time with your son.

Finally, be attentive to the music your son is listening to and to the television shows or movies he is watching. I am amazed at the amount of freedom parents are granting their kids these days. I have mentored several young men under the age of 13 that had cable TV in their rooms and the freedom to listen to just about any music they desired. Let me reiterate that boys are very impressionable. Allowing your son to watch television shows or movies and listen to music that depicts disrespect of women will cancel your efforts to teach him to respect women.

So, how can a mother teach her son to value and respect women? First, she must show him that she values and respects herself. Secondly, she must make sure her son is surrounded by other people who will uphold and support the same values she wants her son to learn. Finally, she must constantly censor such things as music and television that may glorify and promote negative definitions, stereotypes and treatment of women.

Our boys must understand that a woman is not a punching bag. She is not a sexual object and she is not best defined as "a dime piece" or "my baby's mama." But a woman can best be defined as God's improvement to the solitary and incomplete state of man. In the Bible, Genesis 2:18 confirms that God created woman so that man would not be alone. By God, women have been given the important task of making men better as their wife while being the functioning conduit for human life on earth.

Teaching your son how to value and treat a woman starts with you in the home. Before I became a gentleman to others, my mom taught me to do the following for her and my sisters at home:

* Give a lady my seat if she walks into the room.

* Never let a lady carry heavy things when I am around.

* Avoid hitting a lady, even if she hits me.

* Never objectify ladies or their body parts.

* Open doors for ladies.

* Pull out the chair for a lady when seating.

As a mother, you have the power to shape your son's definition of a woman. What will you teach him?

~ Notes ~

~ Notes ~

Chapter Three
Thing 2

A Woman's Job, No Such Thing

One summer day I decided to pick up some of the boys in my mentor program and take them with me to mow yards for the elderly. One of the boys seemed overly anxious to show me he could push the lawn mower and handle the edger. It was his first time mowing lawns with me, and needless to say I was a bit hesitant to trust him with a lawn mower. However, he assured me he could safely handle the equipment. I allowed him the chance to operate the equipment based on his confidence and experience mowing yards with his uncle. He did a great job.

After mowing a few yards, I took the boys home.

As I dropped the young man at his home, his mother invited me in for a minute to chat. While I was conversing with the mother, the young man walked into the living room and told his mother he was hungry. "Can you fix me a sandwich?" he asked. She said okay and proceeded to get up and fix her 11 year old son a sandwich. I thought this was unusual and wanted to say something but didn't.

Fifteen minutes later the young man came back into the living room and told his mother he had some clothes that needed to be washed for the next day. She told him to put the clothes in front of the washing machine; she would wash them later. Again, I wanted to speak out but held my tongue.

A few minutes later I decided to leave. Before leaving, the young man asked me to come into his room to see his pet turtle. The room was a mess. Clothes and toys were spread all over the floor.

As the mother followed me into the room, she began apologizing as she picked up her son's clothes and toys. At that point I had to say something. I asked the mother to walk with me to my car.

While at my car, I explained to her that she was handicapping her son by doing everything for him. Here was a young man who was old enough to operate dangerous lawn equipment but could not fix his own sandwich, wash his own clothes or clean his own room. Afterwards, the mother began to share with me that as a girl she was taught that cooking and cleaning were tasks for women. By doing these things for her son, she thought she was teaching him what to expect in a good woman.

I understood and respected her viewpoint, but what would her son do until he found that good woman? Would he be one of the many young men who lives in a filthy apartment, constantly wears the same dirty clothes and eats fast food for breakfast, lunch and dinner every day?

Since that time, I have witnessed many situations involving mothers who seemingly do everything for their sons. They iron their sons' clothes, prepare their sons' dinner plates and make their sons' beds. One mother I met even ran her 10 year old son's bathwater. I need to get the message out to the mothers that your sons are not your husbands.

Doing all these things for your son may seem harmless. However, the more you do them, the more you add to your son's ignorance. You will actually raise a young man who is capable of many things as long as they are not the things he feels a woman should do.

The truth of the matter is that young men should be given a regular list of chores. These chores should be more than what is considered "boy type" chores such as taking out the trash and raking the yard. Of course you must use wisdom to determine what chores should be assigned to your son according to his age. Yet, I say start assigning chores early.

If he is tall enough to look over the sink, give him the regular task of washing the dishes. If you are like my mother, you can make him start by standing in a chair. Don't hesitate to start him doing the laundry, sweeping, vacuuming, mopping, dusting, ironing or setting the dinner table. I don't recommend giving him an allowance for doing these things. He must learn that these are the everyday chores of life.

In addition to the chores previously mentioned, teach him how to cook. But before doing that, teach him how to make a grocery list, clip discount coupons and shop for food according to brand and value. By teaching him how to do these chores, he will learn that they are not just for women.

Contrary to what some people believe, teaching a boy how to cook and clean does not make him soft. In fact, it is just as important as teaching a young girl how to be independent so she won't have to rely on a man to take care of her. Today's complete man is no longer just defined by his handy man knowledge.

A poll study by **MSN** in 2011 stated that there was an increase in the number of men who enrolled in culinary classes to learn how to cook. It was 20 percent in 2009 but increased to 32 percent in 2011. In an article on **MSN/Today.com**, celebrity chef Marcus Samuelsson stated that being a well-rounded man today means knowing about cooking as well as other "expected" manly duties.

There are many reasons why men should learn how to cook and clean. Most men figure these abilities make them more attractive to women. That may be a true assumption; however, teaching a young man these traits can actually pay off in other ways.

Teaching your son how to shop for groceries and cook those groceries will help him save money on his overall monthly food bill. It's just cheaper to cook meals rather than eat out. I am reminded of my college days when money was extremely tight. I would go to the store and spend $15 on ingredients and make a stew or bake a casserole that would last me half of the week.

I could eat several days for the price of two fast food meals.

Secondly, teaching your son how to cook can contribute to his overall health. It's a proven fact that learning how to cook healthy, balanced meals will help keep your health in check. According to studies done by the **International Food Information Council (IFIC)**, women eat much healthier than men. Studies show that 53 percent of women to 46 percent of men cook and consume specific foods to maintain their overall health. Studies also show that 41 percent of women versus 33 percent of men eat specific foods to improve their digestive health and 34 percent of women versus 27 percent of men eat to improve their energy or stamina.

Thirdly and most importantly, teaching your son how to cook and clean assures his confidence in not being limited to certain abilities just because he is a male. It also shatters any misconceptions that certain tasks are beneath him because he is a male.

Your son will be well on his way to being a well-rounded man. One who can cook and clean without compromising his masculinity.

~ Notes ~

~ Notes ~

Chapter Four
Thing 3

The Importance of Good Personal Hygiene

I was at the barbershop one Saturday afternoon when one of the regular male customers decided to share the intimate details of his date with a woman he met at a club. He said he took the woman out for a romantic dinner and was certain he would be able to seduce her afterwards. After the date, they went back to his place where he proceeded to undress her. As he got her skirt off, he claimed she had a large stain in her underwear. He described the stain as being the same stain that many men have in the seat of their underwear.

Immediately the men in the shop began to speak out with disgust. One of the barbers shouted, "Man, if I get in that situation and a woman has the same stain in her panties as I have in my underwear, that's a nasty woman!" To my surprise, several of the men began to agree with him. The barbershop talk was intensified with grown men talking about how it is acceptable for a man to have stains in his underwear but if a woman has them, it's downright nasty!

Like many times before, I was somewhat ashamed to be a part of the male species. How can a mature man reason that his dirty underwear is somehow cleaner than a woman's dirty underwear? The conversation took me back to a time when I was around 11 or 12 years old. My family had a washer and dryer, and my mother taught my younger sisters and me how to wash our own clothes. My sisters were diligent at the task of keeping their clothes clean. I, on the other hand, was going through that dirty little boy stage.

That's the stage when little boys don't take baths regularly, wear the same dirty clothes several times a week and **DON'T CHANGE THEIR UNDERWEAR EVERYDAY**.

One day I got into trouble and my mother decided to give me a good ole fashioned, pull your pants down whipping. I forget exactly what I did to merit the whipping, but I do remember my mom's face when she made me pull down my pants. Though she was already angry about what I did, seeing that big stain in my underwear infuriated her to the point that the whipping was no longer about what I had done initially. Instead, it was to punish me for wearing filthy underwear.

I will never forget that day. After she whipped me, my mother made me take a bath while she watched. I was so embarrassed. She also warned me that she would be checking regularly to make sure I was taking a bath and changing my underwear daily. To this day, I've NEVER had that problem again! Thinking back on that experience, I doubt my father would have taken such measures to make sure I had learned my lesson.

I don't know why there is a double standard. As men, we presuppose certain nonreciprocal expectations on women. We want them to stay clean and odor free all the time. We want them to have healthy, blemish free, soft, lotioned skin and clean healthy nails. We expect them to have pearly white teeth, and well managed hairstyles. But as men, we excuse ourselves of these responsibilities. Why do we do this? Dirt is dirt! No matter if it's on a woman or a man.

It seems that men who make sure they are neat, clean and well dressed are often labeled as homosexual or metro sexual males. A male friend of mine ridiculed me when he learned that I frequent the nail salon for regular pedicures and/or manicures. He said there is something wrong when a man feels comfortable being pampered like a woman. I tried to explain to him that my trips to the nail salon were not about being pampered. They were simply about taking care of my hands and feet.

I am not surprised by my friend's comment. Like many boys, I was encouraged by the men in my family to ignore those personal hygiene habits that are considered to be more feminine. I remember asking my late grandfather for some lotion once. He laughed and said, "You don't need lotion. We are men. We are supposed to be rugged." I know he meant no harm, but I thank God for my mother, grandmother and a couple of female friends who constantly encouraged me to do a better job at mindful hygiene as I grew up.

It is so important for a young boy to learn good hygiene habits? First of all, it will benefit his overall personal health by creating healthy habits such as washing his hands, bathing, and brushing his teeth regularly. You may be shocked at the number of men who don't practice these things on a regular basis. I have been in bathrooms from coast to coast and witnessed men from janitors to executives use the facilities and walk out without washing their hands.

Secondly, good hygiene habits help guard against social embarrassments such as bad body or foot odor which is common among men. Lastly, good hygiene habits contribute to a better self-image which adds to a person's overall attractiveness and self-confidence.

It's evident by the story at the beginning of this chapter that some women don't practice good hygiene. However, it is because of what society expects from women that most of them do practice better hygiene than men. It is time for men to be held to the same standards they hold women to regarding hygiene. **And as a mother, you can change this double standard beginning with your son.**

~ Notes ~

~Notes ~

Chapter Five
Thing 4

Smart Finances

I was standing in line at the bank one summer afternoon when a woman walked in with her two sons. The boys, whom I later learned were five and three years old, had their piggy banks in hand as they got in line to make a deposit. They seemed to be overly excited to be at the bank with their savings. The line was long and the older boy kept asking his mother how long before they would get to the teller. The mother kept urging him to calm down and told him he would see the teller soon.

I finished taking care of my business and walked over to the waiting area to get a cup of coffee.

I decided to stay at the bank to observe what would happen when the boys made it to the teller window. When they reached the teller, the mother told the older son to show the younger one how to deposit his money. The five year old placed his piggy bank on the teller counter by raising both arms. In an excited voice he said, "Hi, my name is Jonathan, and I want to deposit this money into my savings account, please." The teller asked him if he knew how much money he had in the piggy bank. "Fourteen dollars and nineteen cents," he replied. Then he asked the teller if she could give him a statement with the total amount of money in his savings account. He got his receipt and turned around with the biggest smile on his face. He then helped his mother show his younger brother how to do the same thing.

I was in absolute awe while observing the young boys. The first thing I thought about was that the mother and her two sons were Caucasian. The second thing that ran through my mind was that I was in an upscale part of the city at the time.

The third thing that crossed my mind was how fortunate those young boys were. Their mother, who I found out was a homemaker, was giving them an advantage in life by teaching them this important financial lesson of how to save money and be excited about it.

Now I must admit that the thoughts that raced through my mind while I was in the bank that day have a lot to do with my own financial regrets. I, like many minorities, had to learn about the principles of smart finances the hard way. Unfortunately, I was in my thirties before I really understood the importance of budgeting, saving, investing and maintaining a good credit score. As a mature man, these things are very important to me now, and I often wonder what my financial situation would be if I had been given the same early lessons as those young boys.

There used to be a time when the essence of manhood meant that a "man" had achieved or was striving to achieve certain basic financial status.

A "man" was expected to have his own vehicle and his own place to live. A "man" was expected to have a job or at least put forth efforts to try and find one. A "man" would never feel comfortable relying on his woman to pay his bills and give him money. But over the years these expectations have somehow been deemed unnecessary or unimportant by the majority of society. Much of that majority consist of the women that are mothers, sisters, girlfriends and wives.

I do applaud today's modern women. They are taking care of their business by going to college, getting their degrees and getting the high paying jobs. They have the nice cars, live in nice homes and are doing it all without the help of men. But while women have the drive and determination to strive for personal financial freedoms, they are not requiring that same drive from the men they have relationships with. Today's men are comfortable driving their women's cars, living in their women's houses and spending their women's money.

As a mother, you can help improve this disturbing trend. You must first understand that giving your son everything he asks for is not wise. My experience as a mentor has shown me that many young men don't understand or respect the word NO. I can't count the number of times I picked up young boys from single parent homes and took them places only to find myself telling them "NO" repeatedly. I realized that many of these boys were accustomed to their mothers buying them whatever they asked for while in the store. Their mothers might have told them no at first, but they knew if they kept asking, eventually they would get what they wanted.

One mother explained that she did this because she loved her son and felt sorry that he did not have a father figure in his life. I told her that if she really loved him, she would teach him that most things in life will not be given to him. He must learn to earn things through honest work and understand that sometimes he will have to save money in order to buy some of the things he wants.

If you have good personal financial practices, don't be shy about teaching them to your son. I have noticed that most single mothers today are doing whatever it takes to be better providers for their families. Statistics show that women are beginning to lead the charge in areas of financial importance. An online article by **DailyFinance.com** reported that many studies prove women are better financial planners and investors than men. A recent study by **Experian**, a credit reporting agency, showed that women averaged a better credit score and less debt than men. The same study showed that although women make an average of 23 percent less income than men, they seem to manage that income much more efficiently. **So, who better than mom can teach her young man to be more financially smart?**

~ Notes ~

~ Notes ~

Chapter Six
Thing 5

Be Who You Is

I will never forget being in church one Sunday morning when my late grandfather, Pastor Charles Legardy stepped up to the pulpit when it was time to preach and shouted, "**BE WHO YOU IS!**" And again he shouted, "**BE WHO YOU IS, BECAUSE IF YOU AIN'T WHO YOU IS, YOU IS WHO YOU AINT!**" The saying made many of us in the pews laugh as we tried to accept his serious demeanor while using incorrect grammar. My grandfather knew he was using incorrect grammar, but his goal was to get everyone's attention. The purpose of his message was simply to encourage us Christians to live like Christians and not like heathens.

As a Christian, the power of that message has encouraged me through the years to accept my identity in Christ. However, the same message can also be a good life principal to ALWAYS BE YOURSELF. The saying seems simple enough, but many boys struggle with this concept. I was one of those boys.

I can remember being the age of 11 and having a major crush on a 14 year old girl named Cindy who lived in my apartment complex. She had a younger brother my age, and I made friends with him just so I could be near her when he and I played outside. Cindy knew I liked her but never paid me much attention. She liked older teenage boys. Cindy would let these boys into her apartment when her mother was not at home. Cindy's brother and I would observe as her suitors smoked cigarettes, engaged in vulgar conversations, took off their shirts, wrestled with each other and rapped the popular hip hop music of the time. It seemed as if all of the foolish, macho behavior impressed Cindy. She would kiss and hug the young men after their ridiculous behavior.

After weeks of hoping that Cindy would miraculously notice me as I played outside with my friends, I decided I was tired of waiting. I figured if I was going to make Cindy like me, I had to act like the older boys. So I waited until Cindy came outside on her porch and proceeded on my mission to win her love.

There was only one problem with my plan. My mother just happened to be watching me through a window in our apartment. I never expected her to do that, since the only window that she could observe me from was in my bedroom in the back of the apartment. I later found out that my mother would often watch my sisters and me as we played outside. Yes, my mother was watching me. She watched me as I used profanity. She watched me as I tried to rap secular songs. She watched me as I wrestled some of the other little boys to the ground in front of Cindy.

After watching me make a fool of myself for about an hour, my mother grabbed her belt, came outside on the porch and angrily called me into our apartment.

I didn't know which was worse; looking at my mother and realizing I was in trouble or hearing the laughter of Cindy and the other neighborhood boys as I hurried to the apartment. I will never forget hearing Cindy say, "OOOHH, yo momma about to whoop yo butt."

As I got to the top of the stairs, my mom grabbed my shirt, pushed me into the apartment and shouted, "Boy, have you lost your mind? Why are you outside acting like a fool in front of that girl? I did not teach you to act like that!" I was too embarrassed to tell my mother that I was just trying to impress Cindy, but she knew what I was trying to do.

My little circus act got me put on punishment, but not before my mother had a long talk with me about being myself. She explained to me that anyone can copy another person's behavior, but it takes a strong person to be himself. She also explained that a mature woman will always desire a man who is confident and genuine.

This unforgettable lesson was just one of many that taught me the importance of being myself.

I am fortunate that my mother constantly reminded me of her expectations of me as I grew up. Those expectations, which were rooted in an understanding of what she, considered acceptable and honorable manhood traits, helped shape me into the man that I am today.

A young man who understands the importance of being himself has two major advantages over his peers. The first advantage is the ability to think rationally and make choices for himself. The second advantage is the ability to ignore the pull of acceptance through bad peer pressure. As I stated earlier in this book, boys are very **IMPRESSIONABLE**. Boys who are not taught to develop a healthy self-identity often emulate the behavior of others with no thought of the consequences. These same boys will often do whatever it takes to win the acceptance of their peers, even if it means getting into trouble.

This is the reason why FBI crime statistics have reported that 90 percent of U.S. gangs are made up of males as opposed to 10 percent female.

The FBI also reports that the majority of males who join gangs join between the ages of 9 to 12 and remain in the gang into adulthood. This proves that a large percentage of boys who fail to develop their own self-identity become men who have no self-identity.

The key to guiding your son towards a wholesome self-identity is to first understand what the term "self-identity" means. *Self-identity* is the quality that makes a person the same or different from others. It's important to note both the words "same" and "different." Complete self-identity is made up of two parts, **personal identity** and **social identity**.

Personal identity is defined by a person's individual traits. It is defined by the things that a person is interested or disinterested in. It is also defined by a person's intellect. It is defined by a person's mental and physical attributes. Many of the same common things come together to make up a boy's personal identity.

However, these things are a part of a normal growth process that begins when a boy is very young and ends at different ages according to how fast he matures.

Most boys share certain personal identity traits that may be foreign and annoying to you as a woman. As the saying goes, boys will be boys. Boys like to play in the dirt and get dirty, climb trees, throw rocks and collect bugs and critters. They also like to run and jump, step in water puddles and spit on the ground. They seemingly have no fear and endless energy. They get scrapes and bruises. They wrestle with each other. I can go on and on.

Although these personal identity traits are normal in healthy boys, I've noticed that many mothers do everything they can to discourage these traits. I cannot count the number of times I witnessed a single mother threaten to whip her son for normal boy behavior. Boys will eventually mature out of these behaviors.

When it comes to teaching boys to be themselves, I need mothers to pay less attention to their sons' normal physical behaviors and put more effort into teaching them about their social identities.

Social identity is defined as a person's sense of who they are based on their group membership(s) or the people that they are around. The Theory of Social Identity was introduced in 1979 by Henry Tajfel and John Turner. The theory states that there are three mental processes involved in developing a person's social identity. The first process is *categorization.* Is the person black or white? Is the person a doctor or a lawyer? Is the person a teacher or a preacher? These are all categories that can be used to define people.

Social identification is the second process. This process allows a person to adopt the identity of the group that he has categorized himself as belonging to. If you categorized yourself as a musician, you will more than likely act like you feel a musician should act.

The final process is called **social comparison**. At this point, the person has identified his group category. He now understands what is expected of him and can compare his group and its behavior with other groups and their behaviors.

Understanding this theory allows you to use the same three concepts to shape your son's self-identity.

1.   Who he is (**categorization**) - As his mother, you should start telling him who he is as early as possible. Tell him he is a boy but will one day be a man. Tell him he is God's creation and was born into this world for a positive purpose. Tell him he is a gentleman. Avoid calling him out of his name or using any negative connotations. (Example – you're just like your daddy – no good.)

2.   What is expected of him (**social identification**) – Now that you are telling him who he is, you must also tell him what is expected of him.

Honesty, chivalry, empathy and respect are just a few examples of what may be expected of him. Be prepared to constantly reiterate and reinforce these expectations as he grows up. Take great interest in who he spends time with, the music he listens to, the media/social sites he spends time visiting and the TV shows and movies he watches.

3.   Be who you is (**social comparison**) – As the first two social identity concepts are enacted, your son will begin to develop his own identity. Your success in teaching him who he is and what is expected of him will be evident by the way he governs himself. **He will have the ability to discern what is right and wrong and make life decisions based on his own virtues.**

~ Notes ~

~ Notes ~

Chapter Seven
Thing 6

Teach Civility and Proper Respect Will Follow

One day when I was 12 years old and in sixth grade gym class, I finished my mandatory exercises early and decided to go outside on the basketball court. It was late fall and too cold for any of the other kids to join me outside. I threw the basketball around for about 10 minutes. Afterwards, I went to the locker room to get dressed for my next class. The other boys were also getting dressed.

I dressed quickly and decided to walk to my next class which was on the other side of the school building. I had enjoyed the cool weather so much that I decided to walk the outside route to the class.

As I exited the gym, I proceeded towards the basketball court. The girls' locker room window was adjacent to the court. One of the girls, whom I had a crush on, was standing next to the cracked locker room window getting dressed. The window was only open about 12 inches; however, it was enough for me to see her standing there in her bra and panties. She saw me and quickly stepped away from the window.

The gym window was about five feet high, and it was obvious that this young lady never expected someone to be walking outside in the cold. I immediately ran back inside the boys' locker room. With excitement, I began to tell the other boys that I had just seen this young lady in her bra and panties. Sharing what I saw immediately sent the boys locker room into a frenzy. Some of the boys didn't believe me, but others asked me questions about her anatomy. I was the locker room champion for about five minutes.

I remember leaving the locker room feeling privileged. Every sixth grade boy liked this young lady, but I was the one who saw her in her underwear.

I am not sure what I expected to happen after telling all the boys in the locker room about what I saw. However, I definitely was not prepared for what did happen.

The next day while in one of my morning classes, the school counselor came into the class and whispered in my teacher's ear. The teacher looked at me in disbelief. The counselor, who knew me well, asked me to come with her. I followed her to her office. As I walked in I saw the girl and her parents. At that moment I knew I was in trouble.

It seems like it only took one class period for the information I shared with nine boys in the locker room to spread throughout the school to over 300 students. Not only did the story spread, but it changed from what I reported seeing to stories full of lies. Some of the students told other students that I saw the girl naked. Others said that I saw her fondling herself. The young lady was teased and jeered so much that she had to leave school early that day.

7 Things Every Mother Should Teach Her Son

I had no idea that the situation had gotten so out of hand. The young lady told her parents what happened. Her parents called the school principal who actually lived in the same neighborhood. They told the principal that their daughter was refusing to go back to school. The principal called the counselor. The counselor persuaded the parents to allow her to investigate the matter.

While sitting in the counselor's office the next morning in the presence of the girl and her parents, the counselor asked me what happened. I told her what I did and what I said. I took great care to emphasize that all I did was tell the other boys what I saw. All the stories about the girl being naked and touching herself were made up by other people. I told them I never intended for the girl to get hurt.

The counselor asked me to apologize to the girl and to her parents. The girl began to cry as she and her parents left the office. The counselor looked at me, shook her head and said, "Darrell King, I have always thought highly of you.

60

You are one of the brightest young men in this school. I am shocked at what you did. But because I feel you will learn from this experience, I will not call your mother." Instead, she made me agree to a one hour counseling session with her a week from that day.

A week later I met with the counselor. She asked me if I noticed that many of the school kids were still talking about the incident. "Yes," I replied. "Let me teach you something," she said. "There is a double standard when it comes to men and women. If you decide as a young man to take off your clothes and walk down the school hallway naked, most of the students would laugh at you and consider you to be practical joker. Within a day or two, the incident will be old news. If a young lady did the same thing, she would be ridiculed and talked about for weeks. She would be considered dirty, a whore or a slut. By doing what you did, you subjected that young lady to that same type of ridicule. Her parents have transferred her to another school." I was shocked.

"Wait a minute ma'am! I am not the person to blame for this. I just said what I saw. I never said she was naked. I have too much respect for women to do something like that! Why won't you find the boys who are spreading the lies and make them tell the truth about what I said?"

"Where was your respect when you decided to go back into the locker room and share what you saw? Respect is more than a notion, Mr. King. True respect carries great responsibility! You told me you felt privileged to see this young lady in her underwear.
The word privilege has several definitions, Mr. King. The first definition of privilege is a benefit given to some and not others. However, the second definition of privilege is a special opportunity to do something that makes you proud. In other words, Mr. King, you were privileged in a way to see what you saw by accident. But if you really understood respect, the real privilege, would have been to keep what you saw to yourself. Think about what you did!

Your decision to share something that should have been kept secret has affected a whole family. That young lady can never walk these hallways again without being thought of without her clothes on. Put yourself in the place of that young lady. How would you feel if someone selfishly took advantage of your most embarrassing moments?"

At that point my mindset changed. I was no longer trying to think of ways to defend my actions. As I thought about what I did, what it caused and how it all could have been avoided, I realized how irresponsible my actions were. In one hour the counselor introduced me to the concept of civility. I learned that I had a moral responsibility to be trustworthy, to show empathy, compassion and to practice self-control.

After years as a youth pastor and mentor, I have come to understand that you cannot effectively teach your son respect without first teaching him the concept of civility. Attempting to do so is often a waste of time.

Over the years I have lent a crying shoulder to many single mothers with sons who were either incarcerated, on drugs or constantly in trouble for delinquent activity. Many of these mothers found themselves wondering where they went wrong in raising their sons. I can't count the number of times I have heard a mother say, "I don't know what happened to him. I tried my best to teach him respect."

For the most part, single moms have the right idea. It is very important for a boy to learn the proper concept of respect. But respect in all its glory has a major weakness. The weakness is that respect is open to individual interpretation. Respect by definition can be a noun or a verb. As a noun, respect is defined as a feeling of admiring someone or something that is good, valuable, important, etc. As a verb, respect is defined as the act of esteeming or holding someone or something in high regard.

Most boys are introduced to the word as a verb without being taught the full definition of the word as a noun.

If you do not teach them the full context of the word, they will often decide who to respect based on their own interpretation. This is why many boys today respect drug dealers, pimps, murderers and rappers. Unfortunately, their respect for these individuals will often influence their behavior.

Civility is training in the humanities. If you teach a boy the concept of civility, you are teaching him how to be polite, reasonable and respectful to his fellow man. Civility is Respect's big brother. It keeps respect in line. It helps boys know who to respect and how to respect. Boys that are taught the concept of civility grow up understanding that they have a duty to be a positive influence in society.

When it comes to teaching civility, it appears that women have the upper hand over men. In a recent study entitled **"Women, Men, and Civility,"** women did better than men in EVERY area of study. The study showed women to be more polite, less likely to insult others and more attentive listeners.

If you want to raise a boy who will embody proper respect, start by teaching him civility.

~ Notes ~

~ Notes ~

Chapter Eight
Thing 7

A Personal Relationship with God

One of my most awakening moments as a youth minister happened in 2009. Several of the young people in the youth ministry class graduated from high school that year. Most of them had been under my spiritual teaching for five to six years. Once they graduated from high school, they also graduated from the youth ministry and started attending adult church.

In one of my last ministry sessions with the graduates, I decided to give a recap of what I thought was some of my most important youth ministry lessons. I urged the graduates to remember what I taught them regarding sexual immorality, submitting to authority, using profanity, drinking alcohol and using drugs.

After the session, one of my favorite students allowed the room to clear and walked up to me. "I want to tell you something," the student said. "I want you to know that I intentionally lost my virginity after the prom last week. I debated whether to call you the night before the prom, but I knew you would try to talk me out of it. I know what you have taught me about premarital sex since middle school, but I got tired of waiting and wanted to experience it. I hope you are not disappointed in me."

I was completely taken aback by what I heard. It took me a minute to realize this was not a joke. This was one of my best Bible students. This student always brought their bible to the youth ministry, always volunteered to pray us in or out of service and supported me when I had to debate a point with the students who were not so tolerant of my opinion.

Of all my Bible students, I would not have expected this one to intentionally ignore my biblical teaching. My mind was full of questions. I wondered where did I go wrong?

I began to think about the countless times I showed videos and invited guests to speak to the students about the dangers of drug use and premarital sex. I thought about all the research, energy and preparation I put into teaching (out of the box) lessons on biblical commandments. And amid all that teaching, some of my young Bible students were still being sidelined by the very things I passionately exposed and taught against. How in the world could this happen?

A few days later I was studying Romans 3. During that time, I came across verse 23. The verse reads, "For all have sinned and come short of the glory of God." I had read this passage several times, but this time it awakened my understanding to the fact that all of us are born into the world with a sin nature. This sin nature or desire to sin is just as strong, if not stronger, in kids as it is in adults. I immediately realized that although I was teaching my students relevant biblical lessons of importance, I was ignoring their spiritual needs.

My focus should have been less on right and wrong Christian behavior and more on how to cultivate a personal relationship with God through Jesus Christ.

It may seem like both behavior and relationship are one in the same, but they are not. **Kids are simply young sinners**. Teaching them biblical rules and commandments will educate them but has little power alone to help them make spiritually conscious decisions. After studying this verse, I realized that it was naïve of me to think that the young people in the youth ministry would somehow avoid sin based on their respect for me and my expectations of them.

All of the (things) discussed in the previous chapters of this book will help your son grow to become a well-rounded man, but it will be his personal relationship with God through salvation (and not your expectations) that will constantly keep him on the right path. Teaching your son to cultivate his relationship with God is in fact the greatest thing you can teach him.

Apart from acting as a progressive deterrent to sinful acts, salvation will bring him into fellowship with God. As he grows in Christian knowledge, God's expectations will increasingly become paramount to him. Therefore, God's expectations of him will help govern his conduct.

Teaching your son about salvation should be the responsibility of both parents. With no father in the home, the task falls on you. But be encouraged. Statistics are confirming that women are the true heavy weights when it comes to Christianity. Below are the stats reported by churchformen.org and The Washington Area Coalition of Men's Ministries (WACMM.)

* U.S. church attendance draws a crowd made up of 61 percent female to 39 percent male.
* Thirteen million more women attend church than men on any given Sunday.
* Nearly 25 percent of married, churchgoing women will worship without their husbands on Sunday.

* Midweek services and church activities often draw 70 to 80 percent female participants.

* The majority of church employees are women (except for ordained clergy, who are overwhelmingly male.)

These are just a few of the statistics that show how much of a major role women play in the church today. On one hand, the statistics are disturbing as they point out the massive weakness and decline of men in Christianity. On the other hand they support my opinion that women can teach the principles of salvation as good as any man can.

In order to properly teach your son about salvation, you must be able to answer three questions.

1.   What is salvation? Salvation has several different denominational viewpoints and requirements. If you were to look the definition up in most dictionaries, you will find a definition that reads similar to this.

Salvation is the deliverance of sinful mankind by the grace of God, from eternal punishment or spiritual death for sin which is granted to those people who accept by faith, God's conditions of repentance and faith in the Lord Jesus. This definition might make sense to you, but it will probably be very confusing to your son. My experience as a youth pastor has taught me that most young people think of salvation as an enemy to their fun and free lifestyle. They figure it should be reserved for the time they become an adult. They think this way because in many denominations salvation is often championed as a life of constant prayer, Bible reading, fasting, going to church and denying yourself until you either die or the Rapture takes place. As a mother, your task is to introduce salvation to your son in a way that makes it attractive and attainable. I suggest that you start simply explaining to your son by the time he is two or three years old that Salvation is a personal relationship with Christ. Your son will begin to learn and comprehend the more complex details of salvation as he gets older.

2.   Why do I need salvation? This is can be a tricky question to answer. Most kids that attend church understand basic principles about Christianity. They understand from an early age who God and Jesus are. They know from being taught in Sunday School and Children's Church that Jesus died for their sins. As a mother with the task of teaching your son why he needs salvation, again my advice is to keep it simple. Even if your son is under the age of five, you should start telling him that we were all born sinners. If he is old enough to comprehend the story of Adam and Eve, then explain Adam's mistake in the Garden of Eden (Genesis.) Then explain that we need salvation because as sinners it helps us to live in a way that is pleasing to God. This advice is to mothers who have very young sons. Older boys will understand a more mature answer to this question. Therefore, use the wisdom you have of your son's aptitude to learn accordingly.

3.   How do I obtain salvation? You start off teaching your son simple things about salvation. But it is extremely important to allow him to come to Christ in his own time. When he is ready, he will most likely let you know that he wants to be saved. This is called the age of accountability, and it happens at different ages in young people. A child that wants to be saved may be a bit confused about the actual act of conversion. Therefore, it is important to teach him that there is no way anyone can pay for the free gift of salvation. However, in order to obtain salvation, we must first admit in our hearts that we are sinners. Next, we admit that we believe in Jesus and the sacrifice He made for us on the cross. Finally, we accept the free gift, not because we deserve it, but because we need it.

Let me conclude by admitting that this chapter is nowhere close to being as detailed as it could be. My intention is not to try to teach you to be an expert in youth ministry.

It is simply to suggest a workable plan of ideas that will prayerfully contribute to raising a spiritually sound and by most definitions, great young man. But before I close this chapter, I need to make two very important points.

To the mothers who have a personal relationship with Christ. I urge you to be mindful of your walk with Christ in front of your sons at all times. It is unfortunate for me to admit that much of the crazy, and sometimes incorrect behaviors I have witnessed while mentoring son's of single mothers is from mothers who are Christians. No one is perfect, but the more you adhere to or obey God's word in front of your son, the better he will be.

To the mothers who are reading this book and are not Christians, I cannot express the importance of your salvation. You cannot teach your son about something that you don't know. What you do and say will be noticed and accepted by your son from birth. As his mother, you can influence him in a positive or negative way.

There are many mothers today who live immoral lives full of perversion. As they verbalize profanities, use drugs, get drunk and fornicate, they normalize these things to their sons better than any outside influence can. If you don't have a relationship with God, stop right now and ask Him to forgive you for your sins. Confess that you believe that God sent His son Jesus to die for you, and that Jesus died and rose again on the third day. Then ask God to come into your heart. You are now saved. Find a Bible based Christian church for you and your son to join and move forward in life.

In closing, allow me to encourage you again as a mother to stop making excuses. Stop wondering why this task of raising your son was solely left to you. Stop allowing bitter thoughts about your son's father to sideline and/or distract you. And finally, stop thinking that the task is too much for you to handle. **No matter the circumstances involved in your situation, you have a son to raise. With God's help, you will teach him how to be a true man you can be proud of.**

May God richly bless you!

Minister Darrell King

~ Notes ~

~ Notes ~

Bibliography

~ Book References ~

The King James Bible

The New International Bible

~ Web References ~

FBI.Gov

Researchgate.net

Newser.com

EducationPortal.com

SafeHorizon.org

ClarkProsecutor.org

DailyFinance.com

Experian.com

MSN.com

MSNToday.com

Wikipedia.org